AMERICAN INDIAN ART AND CULTURE
The Navajo

RENNAY CRAATS

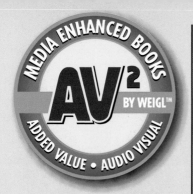

AV² provides enriched content that supplements and complements this book. Weigl's AV² books strive to create inspired learning and engage young minds in a total learning experience.

Your AV² Media Enhanced books come alive with...

 Audio
Listen to sections of the book read aloud.

 Key Words
Study vocabulary, and complete a matching word activity.

 Video
Watch informative video clips.

 Quizzes
Test your knowledge.

Go to **www.av2books.com**, and enter this book's unique code.

 Embedded Weblinks
Gain additional information for research.

 Slide Show
View images and captions, and prepare a presentation.

BOOK CODE

Y 5 2 2 3 4 8

 Try This!
Complete activities and hands-on experiments.

AV² by Weigl brings you media enhanced books that support active learning.

... and much, much more!

Published by AV² by Weigl
350 5th Avenue, 59th Floor
New York, NY 10118

Websites: www.av2books.com   www.weigl.com

Library of Congress Cataloging-in-Publication Data
Craats, Rennay.
 The Navajo / Rennay Craats.
    pages cm. -- (American Indian art and culture)
Originally published: 2004.
Includes bibliographical references and index.
 ISBN 978-1-4896-2914-2 (hard cover : alk. paper) -- ISBN 978-1-4896-2915-9 (soft cover : alk. paper) -- ISBN 978-1-4896-2916-6 (single user ebook) -- ISBN 978-1-4896-2917-3 (multi-user ebook)
1. Navajo Indians--History--Juvenile literature. 2. Navajo Indians--Social life and customs--Juvenile literature. I. Title.
 E99.N3C789 2014
 979.1004'9726--dc23
                    2014038977

Printed in the United States of America in Brainerd, Minnesota
1 2 3 4 5 6 7 8 9 18 17 16 15 14

122014
WEP051214

Project Coordinator: Heather Kissock
Design: Terry Paulhus

Every reasonable effort has been made to trace ownership and to obtain permission to reprint copyright material. The publishers would be pleased to have any errors or omissions brought to their attention so that they may be corrected in subsequent printings.

Weigl acknowledges Getty Images as its primary image supplier for this title.

Contents

The People

The Navajo traveled from what is now Canada to the present-day United States between 1200 and 1500. They moved from place to place around the Southwest, hunting animals and gathering food. They also raided **Pueblo** farming settlements. The Navajo first encountered the Spanish and the Mexicans in the 1600s. The Navajo received horses, goats, and sheep from the Spanish. The Mexicans taught the Navajo silversmithing. The Pueblo shared their weaving and pottery-making techniques. These skills changed the Navajo's way of life.

By the late 1800s, conflict erupted between the U.S. government and the Navajo. In 1863, U.S. forces destroyed Navajo homes and crops, and took their livestock. Thousands of Navajo were captured or forced to surrender. The captives were made to walk to a reservation at Fort Sumner, New Mexico. Their **deportation** is known as the "Long Walk." Many people died along the 300-mile (483-kilometer) trek. In 1868, a **treaty** was signed, which allowed the surviving Navajo to return to their territory, where a new **reservation** had been built.

The Navajo learned shepherding from the Spanish.

Today, the Navajo are one of the largest American Indian groups in the United States. More than 60 **clans** live in Arizona, Colorado, New Mexico, and Utah. About 285,000 Navajo live on reservation land. This land is called the Navajo Nation. The Navajo try to find ways to balance modern culture with their traditional ways. Many Navajo work in cities, in careers such as medicine, education, and law. However, they still recognize the beliefs of their **elders**.

NAVAJO MAP

Location of the Navajo reservation in Arizona, Utah, and New Mexico

Legend
- Navajo communities

0   100 Miles

100 Kilometers

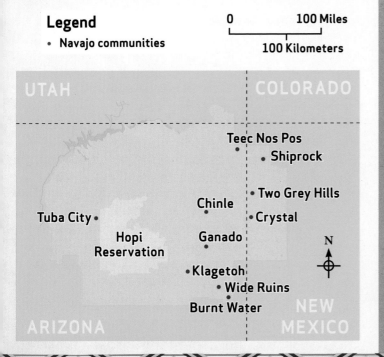

UTAH

COLORADO

Teec Nos Pos

Shiprock

Two Grey Hills

Chinle

Crystal

Tuba City

Ganado

Hopi
Reservation

N

Klagetoh

Wide Ruins

Burnt Water

ARIZONA

NEW
MEXICO

HUNTING, GATHERING, AND FARMING

The name **Navajo** comes from a Pueblo Indian word for "**planted fields**" or "**farmlands**."

Navajo **women herded sheep** and **goats** after they were introduced by the **Spanish** in the **1600s**.

Sheep and **goats** were used for **milk, meat,** and **wool.**

Navajo **women** were responsible for **farming.** They grew **corn, squash, beans,** and **melons.**

Navajo men were responsible for hunting. They hunted **rabbits**, prairie dogs, **deer**, elk, antelope, and bighorn sheep.

Navajo Homes

The first Navajo who arrived in what is now the United States did not need permanent houses. They were **nomadic**. The Navajo did not stay in one place for very long. They moved to areas where there were many animals to hunt. When they learned to farm and raise livestock, the Navajo built permanent communities. They built homes called **hogans**. Each hogan housed an extended Navajo family. The first **fork-stick** hogans were cone-shaped homes that had five sides. The Navajo covered hogans with mud and bark to protect them from the weather. In areas where winters were cold, clay or mud walls were made thicker for extra protection. Hearth fires heated hogans. A hole at the top of the hogan allowed smoke from the fires to escape.

In some areas, Navajo families still live in hogans, especially during the summer.

DWELLING AND DECORATION

A short, covered passage attached to the eastern side of the hogan served as the building's entrance, which always faced the rising Sun. The Navajo carefully considered where to build each hogan. They would not build on gravesites, old battlegrounds, or areas where trees had been struck by lightning.

The introduction of the railroad in the early 1900s made large supplies of building materials, such as wooden crossties, available. This allowed the Navajo to construct larger, taller hogans, which had six or eight sides.

Today, hogans have one round room that is about 23 feet (7 meters) across. These large buildings are most often used for ceremonies and **curings**. Ceremonial hogans can be as large as 50 feet (15.2 m) wide. These structures are the center of the Navajo's spiritual lives.

Many Navajo families who now live in modern homes still have a traditional hogan for ceremonies. Some hogans are used as chapels.

Navajo Communities

After spending years as hunter-gatherers, the Navajo learned another way of life when they met the Pueblo peoples. The Pueblo taught the Navajo how to plant crops. In the 1600s, the Navajo also adopted the Pueblo peoples' practice of raising livestock. Sheep became very important to the Navajo's survival. Sheep provided meat for food as well as wool to make blankets and clothing.

The Navajo traveled to neighboring communities where they traded handmade goods for canned foods, tools, and other manufactured items. The Navajo produced well-known goods, such as baskets, blankets, and rugs. Some settlers visited the Navajo reservation's trading posts to buy these handmade crafts.

Hubbell Trading Post is the oldest continuously operating trading post in the Navajo Nation. It is also a National Historic Site, which means it is a protected area of national historic significance.

Over time, life for the Navajo has changed. Many Navajo have left reservation land to live and work in surrounding cities. The discovery of oil and other minerals, such as uranium, on reservation land has boosted the Navajo Nation's economy. The Navajo Nation Council was established to govern these resources as well as life on the reservation. This council is the largest American Indian government in the United States. It creates laws and decides on punishments for individuals who break these laws.

The Navajo are still well known for their detailed pottery, blankets, and silver jewelry. Techniques for making these items have been passed on from earlier generations.

MODERN LIVING

Today, more than **330,000 Navajo** live in the **United States.**

Navajo **reservation land** covers **24,000** square miles (62,160 square kilometers).

The Navajo Nation is the largest American Indian Nation in the United States.

Many **modern** Navajo still speak the Navajo language.

The **Navajo's** name for themselves is **Diné**, which means "**the people.**"

In **1968**, the Navajo founded **Diné College** in **Arizona. It** is the **first college run** by and for **American Indians.**

Navajo Clothing

Many Navajo honor their culture by wearing traditional clothing. Both men and women wear moccasins. These hard-soled boots can be worn short or knee-high. They are often decorated with colorful beads or detailed **embroidery**. Moccasins are made in a variety of colors and with such materials as buckskin, leather, and suede. The top of the moccasins are often folded over. The Navajo were known to carry knives and other small items in these folds.

Traditionally, Navajo women wore basic skirts made from antelope, deer, or buffalo skins. They made dresses by sewing together woven blankets. Beads or fringe were used to decorate the clothing. Women eventually began trading deerskins and weaving wool for cotton shawls and other European clothes.

In the past, Navajo men wore anklelength, leather leggings and buckskin loincloths. During the winter months, men wore long-sleeved buckskin shirts. The men were also influenced by other cultures. The neighboring Pueblo peoples introduced the Navajo to long pants. Many Navajo men also began wearing Mexican-inspired styles. For example, they wore blankets over one shoulder and mid-calf pants that had silver buttons down each side.

Over time, Navajo styles were replaced with American- and European-inspired clothing, such as velvet, wool, or cotton skirts and blouses.

ADORNMENTS

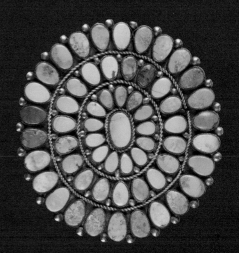

Today, many Navajo combine traditional clothing with modern fashions. While many Navajo men wear blue jeans and cowboy boots, some wear Navajo turquoise jewelry. The Navajo still add detailed embroidery and beadwork to their clothing. Men, women, and children continue to wear traditional clothing for ceremonies and other special occasions.

The Navajo also combine traditional ways of wearing their hair with modern styles. For example, some wear their hair in a traditional bun. Others wear their hair loose, or they wear it in braids for **powwows** or ceremonies.

Navajo Food

Once the Navajo became farmers and shepherds, their diet changed. They no longer needed to hunt game and gather plants. Instead, they ate the animals they raised and the crops they harvested. **Mutton** and goat were valuable food sources. The Navajo also ate beans, corn, and squash.

Navajo diets did not include many dairy products. Many Navajo were **lactose-intolerant**. Instead of drinking milk, the Navajo ate juniper ash, which contained calcium, to keep their bones strong. To create juniper ash, the Navajo burned juniper branches and ground the ashes into a powder. The Navajo then added the powder to traditional breads and blue cornmeal dishes.

Traditional Navajo recipes are passed down from mother to daughter. Many Navajo recipes have never been recorded. The Navajo have always cooked from memory, using their fingers and hands to measure ingredients. Navajo cooks use plants and vegetables, such as cactus, cedar brush, and onions, to make dishes unique.

Mutton and hominy stew with fry bread is an example of traditional Navajo food.

RECIPE

Navajo Fry Bread

Ingredients:

- 2 cups flour
- 1 tablespoon baking powder
- 1 teaspoon salt
- 1 tablespoon vegetable oil
- 3/4 cup warm water
- oil for frying
- powdered sugar, honey, or honey butter

Equipment:

- large bowl
- plastic bag
- wooden spoon
- rolling pin
- wok or deep skillet
- tongs or slotted spatula
- paper towels

Directions

1. Mix dry ingredients together. Stir in oil and water. Mix well.

2. Knead lightly for 1 minute. Do not work the dough too much.

3. Shape the dough into a ball. Put the dough ball in a plastic bag and refrigerate for 1 hour.

4. Remove the dough ball from the refrigerator. Pinch off 12 small balls of dough and flatten each into 3- or 4-inch (7.6- or 10-centimeter) circles. Roll each circle. The thinner the dough circles, the better they will puff in the oil.

5. Poke a hole in the center of each circle with your finger.

6. Dust the tops of the circles with flour while the oil heats in a wok or deep skillet to 375° F. One at a time, place the circles into the hot oil and brown for about 1 minute on each side. Use the tongs or slotted spatula to turn the circles.

7. Dry each circle on paper towels then top with powdered sugar, honey, honey butter, or your favorite topping, and enjoy.

Tools, Weapons, and Defense

Tools helped to make life easier for the Navajo. Many tools, such as ladles, spoons, and dishes, were used every day. These tools were often made from dried gourds or carved from wood.

The Navajo used tools to harvest and prepare corn. They dried corn in order to preserve it for use throughout the year. First, corn was placed in a pot of water over hot coals overnight. Then, in the morning, the corn kernels were scraped from the cob and placed in the Sun to dry. Finally, the Navajo used two pieces of stone to grind the dried kernels into cornmeal.

When making cornmeal, a *mano*, or tube-like stone, was rubbed against a flat stone called the *metate* to grind the kernels.

WEAVING LOOMS AND HUNTING ARROWS

The Navajo were well known for their woven rugs, which also required special tools. To make rugs, the Navajo used upright **looms** and **spindlewhorls** to twist threads together. This created stronger fibers for weaving.

The Navajo used tools to make silver jewelry, too. First, they carved designs into a soft rock. They used the carved rock as a mold to **cast** silver. Navajo jewelers used **awls** to punch designs into the silver pieces. Later, fine files and other tools allowed Navajo silversmiths to make more refined markings.

The bow and arrow was an important weapon for Navajo warriors. The Navajo did not have access to quality hardwood, so their bows were shorter than those made by other American Indian groups. They made arrows from plant shoots and ram horns. The horns were drilled, sanded, and polished to form arrow shafts. The Navajo collected arrowheads from abandoned **pueblo** villages. They could also make arrows from flint. The bow and arrow was a useful hunting tool, which helped make the Navajo a successful people.

Other weaving tools included rods and sticks that were used to separate threads and weave designs into fabric.

Navajo Religion

Religion is an important part of Navajo life. All occasions, from daily life to seasonal responsibilities, are celebrated. For example, rituals are performed to ask the spirits for help during a hunt. The Navajo also bless hogans when they are built.

The Navajo religion is based on a number of gods who are associated with items found in nature. These gods influence the happenings in the Navajo Nation. The Navajo believe in good and evil ghosts. They believe that, in order to have peace and harmony in the world, there must be a strong connection between Earth's different elements. The Navajo honor spirits through ceremonies and daily prayer in order to keep this balance.

American Indians have used peyote in spiritual ceremonies for thousands of years.

The Native American Church (NAC) is an American Indian religion that is popular among some Navajo peoples. The religion is based on drinking or eating the peyote cactus bud. According to this religion, the peyote holds the heart, soul, and memory of the Creator. Eating peyote is thought to bring the individual and the Creator together.

Medicine men and women use a variety of herbs to help heal people.

HOLY LAND

Navajo religion includes several sacred places where the religion must be practiced. Four mountains—Blanca Peak in Colorado, Mount Taylor in New Mexico, the San Francisco Peaks in Arizona, and Hesperus Peak in Colorado—are sacred to the Navajo. They believe the Creator placed Navajo people between these four posts, and they should never leave this holy homeland.

Shiprock in New Mexico is a sacred landform to the Navajo. Its Navajo name means "rock with wings," and refers to the legend of the great bird that carried the Navajo to their present lands.

Ceremonies and Celebrations

The Navajo perform more than 50 different ceremonies throughout the year. Some ceremonies explain events that occur in nature. The *Keshjee'*, or Shoe Game, is one such sacred ceremony that explains the origins of day and night.

A healing ceremony controls dangerous powers and balances a person's physical and spiritual self. Each healing ceremony is different. Chants and rituals are chosen based on the patient's specific problem. Healing ceremonies can last more than one week. Each day of the ceremony, a different song or chant is performed to help cure the patient.

Special mixtures of herbs and other sacred items are used in healing ceremonies.

The Navajo perform ceremonies as part of their daily lives, too. New buildings are blessed with prayers. Sometimes, songs, chants, dances, costumes, and sandpaintings are included as part of these ceremonies. The Navajo House Blessing Ceremony is called *hooghan da ashdlisigil*. This event brings balance, harmony, good luck, and well-being to the people living in the house. The Navajo believe the ceremony will also block bad dreams, evil spirits, hardship, and sickness from entering the house.

The Basket Dance tells the story of the important role of the basket in Navajo life.

Music and Dance

Music is a powerful part of Navajo culture. It is an important part of special ceremonies, as well as daily events. Song lyrics tell stories about Navajo history and life. These songs are passed down orally, so the narrative, or story, is repeated many times. This makes it easier to learn and remember the song. Usually, the Nation's chief leads the singing. Songs are believed to possess healing powers, and many Navajo sing to bring about a desired event.

Most Navajo music is in the form of chants that are performed during ceremonies. Bells, drumbeats, and rattles keep detailed rhythms in time. Ceremonial singing is intended to cure illness. The length of a healing chant varies, depending on the illness it is designed for. Since some ceremonies can last for several days, a chant can include more than 500 songs and thousands of lines.

Traditional Navajo hand drums are made from elk hide. The head of the drum is laced to a frame hoop using a pattern that represents the four directions—north, south, east, and west.

Navajo dancers often act out myths and legends.

CEREMONIAL DANCING

The Navajo perform the *Yeibichai* songs during the nightway ceremony. The nightway ceremony calls upon the *Yeis*, a group of Holy People, to help the Navajo restore harmony. A team of 14 dancers perform the Yeibachai dance before dawn. Dancers wear masks and attach fox pelts to their belts. The dancers remove their masks during the event to show children that they are not **supernatural** beings.

Many Navajo ceremonies feature traditional dancing. Dancers' costumes and masks represent spirits, gods, and animals. One important ritual is the fire dance, or mountainway dance. Participants lunge at each other with firebrands as they dance. Clowns, who are used to bring rain, are also a common feature of the fire dance and nightway ceremony.

Clowns in the fire dance have clay and ash smeared over their skin.

Language and Storytelling

The Navajo language is part of the Athapaskan language family. The Athapaskan language was developed in what is now northwestern Canada and is related to the languages spoken by the Hupa and the Apache peoples. The Navajo language is complicated. One Navajo word can have many meanings. A slight change in the **pronunciation** of a word changes its meaning. The Navajo language contains many unusual sounds. The Navajo sounds "tt," "t'," "ts'," "k'," and "ch'" cannot be translated into English. This makes it difficult for people of other cultures to learn and remember the Navajo language.

For hundreds of years, the Navajo language was only spoken. When **linguists** began recording the Navajo language, they wrote the words exactly as they sounded when they were spoken. Today, the Navajo have both a written and spoken language. Still, many of their stories are passed on orally.

Ancient rock art was also used by the Navajo to tell both stories of historical battles and myths and legends.

Storytellers pass on the Navajo culture and tradition to younger generations. Navajo stories explain the history of the Navajo and how they have evolved. Many stories share common themes and patterns.

One common pattern is the use of the number four. Four represents the seasons, the directions, and the sacred mountains surrounding the Navajo homeland. The number four is also present in tales about mythological figures. These stories have been told for centuries.

Many students in Navajo regions now have the option of attending schools that teach Navajo values, culture, and language alongside regular school subjects.

LAUGHTER

Laughter and humor are an important part of the Navajo language. The First Laugh rite is one example of how humor and laughter are celebrated in the Navajo culture. The first time a Navajo baby laughs aloud is considered cause for a celebration and feast. The person who made the child laugh is honored during the celebration.

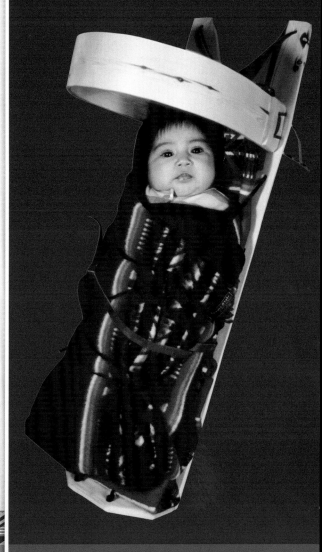

◆ Navajo Art

Most of today's Navajo arts and crafts are linked to Navajo traditions and religion. Navajo women have been expert weavers since the 1600s. The Navajo used sheep's wool to create rugs and blankets. Today, weavers mix creative patterns with traditional designs. Patterns and colors are named according to where they are made, such as Wide Ruins and Chinle.

Sandpainting, or dry painting, is an art form and a ceremonial practice. These pieces of art are most often used during healing ceremonies. Medicine men and women create sandpaintings using colored sands and finely ground charcoal, cornmeal, pollen, and colored rocks. The patient then sits on the completed painting. The Navajo believe sandpaintings absorb evil spirits. The evil spirits will harm the Navajo if the painting is not destroyed. The painting is created and destroyed between sunrise and sunset.

Navajo baskets are usually woven from **sumac**. Navajo weavers begin a basket by making a coil or knot. Then, they wind the sumac around the outer edge of the coil or knot.

Ceremonial baskets are called *Ts'aa'*. Ts'aa' are used to hold objects such as **prayersticks** or **medicine bundles** during rituals. They hold food during a wedding ceremony or ground clay, red **ochre**, and cornmeal during the *kinaalda'*, a coming of age ceremony.

Baskets are very important to the Navajo. The materials and designs used, and even the way in which a basket is made, tells important stories about Navajo values and beliefs.

ART FORMS

Traditional ceremonial baskets have an **opening** from the center of the design to the outer edge. This is called **"the way out."** It represents the spiritual journey from **one world** to the **next.**

To create **silver** pieces, Navajo artists **melted** down U.S. silver dollar **coins** and **Mexican pesos.**

According to Navajo tradition, *Spider Man*, one of the **Holy People**, made the first loom from **sunshine**, lightning, and **rain.**

The Navajo believe that the **Holy People** gave them the **knowledge of sandpainting.**

Sandpaintings can show ceremonies, sacred songs, and spiritual figures.

Code Talkers

During World War II, the **Allies** used the Navajo language to create a code that the Japanese army could not understand. This was a critical development as many earlier codes had been broken by the Japanese. By using the Navajo code, the U.S. Marines were able to communicate with each other without the enemy knowing what they were planning.

In 1942, Navajo marine recruits began working on codes. Navajo marines created a dictionary of military words and terms. They could encode, send, and decode a three-line message in 20 seconds. Before the Navajo code, machines took 30 minutes to encode and then decode the same text. With their oral tradition, the Navajo code talkers found it easy to remember and pass on detailed instructions without writing them down.

A code talker translated a collection of unrelated Navajo words into English. Combining the first letters of each English word spelled out a message. For example, the Navajo word *wol-la-chee* means "ant." It represented the letter "A." About 450 common military words were also translated into Navajo code words. For example, the Navajo used *besh-lo*, which means "iron fish," to represent a submarine, and *dah-he-tih-hi*, which means "hummingbird," to refer to a fighter plane.

The Navajo code talkers sent and received messages using portable radios.

WINDTALKERS

The **secret name** for the Navajo **marines** was **Windtalkers.**

421
Navajo completed **Windtalker training.**

At the beginning of World War II, only **30 non-Navajo** could understand the **language**.

The Navajo language has been described as sounding like the **rumble of a train.**

DECLASSIFIED
TOP SECRET

The **code** was **finally made public** in **1968.**

STUDYING THE NAVAJO'S PAST

Many **anthropologists** and **archaeologists** believe the Navajo first **migrated** to what is now Canada from Asia. They believe the Navajo traveled to the southwestern United States between 1400 and 1500—about the same time Spanish colonists arrived in what is now the United States. However, oral histories told by Navajo storytellers suggest their people arrived in the southwestern United States between 900 and 1130.

Tree-ring dating supports the Navajo's claim. In this method of dating artifacts and events, scientists study tree ring growth to determine when past events occurred or artifacts were made. This dating method suggests hogan-style homes found in Colorado date back to the 1100s.

Archaeologists study pottery and other ancient objects to learn more about the development of a people.

Timeline

First Recorded Contact with Europeans

1500s

Spanish explorer Francisco Vasquez de Coronado first met the Navajo in New Mexico in 1541. In 1583, the first Spanish colonists encountered the Navajo.

Conflict Between Navajo and Other Groups

1600s

Conflict grew between Spanish and American Indian groups. Many Navajo were forced into slavery. The Navajo raided other American Indian villages and Spanish settlements.

Navajo Herding Lifestyle Begins

1630—1680

The Navajo began to herd sheep and horses.

A **homestead** with Navajo features discovered south of Gallup, New Mexico, dated back to 1380. Many of these findings suggest the Navajo lived in the southwestern United States during the same period as the Pueblo peoples.

Scientists do not know exactly when the Navajo journeyed to their current home. Scientists need to collect more ancient artifacts to establish a definite time line. Many experts agree that the Navajo arrived between 800 and 1500.

Canyon de Chelly National Monument, located on Navajo Nation land in Arizona, contains several well-preserved ancient Navajo cliff-dwelling sites.

The Long Walk
1863

The U.S. government took thousands of Navajo people captive. These people were forced to make the Long Walk to Fort Sumner, New Mexico.

Treaty with U.S. Government
1868

A treaty established Navajo reservation land and a peace agreement between the Navajo and the U.S. government.

Navajo Nation Council
1923

The Navajo Nation Council was established.

QUIZ

1 Where do experts believe the Navajo originally came from?

A. Asia

2. What is the deportation of the Navajo by the U.S. government in 1863 called?

A. The Long Walk

3 What are traditional Navajo homes called?

A. Hogans

4 Which Navajo art form is also used during healing ceremonies?

A. Sandpainting, or dry painting

5 Which American Indian people taught the Navajo how to plant crops?

A. The Pueblo

6 Which animal became very important to the Navajo's survival?

A. Sheep

7 How many Navajo live on reservations today?

A. About 285,000

8 How many different ceremonies do the Navajo perform throughout the year?

A. More than 50

9 Which number is often featured in Navajo stories?

A. Four

10 What were Navajo code talkers known as?

A. Windtalkers

KEY WORDS

Allies: a group of countries that fought together during World War II

anthropologists: scientists who study human origins, development, customs, and beliefs

archaeologists: scientists who study objects from the past to learn about past civilizations

awls: sharp tools used for making holes in soft materials

cast: to make something by pouring hot metal into a mold and allowing it to harden

clans: groups of families that are related to each other

curings: healings

deportation: removing a person or people from a region or country

elders: older, influential members of a family or group

embroidery: decorated with needlework

fork-stick: several logs placed in a tent-like formation

hogans: pyramid-shaped homes with five to eight sides

homestead: a house, particularly a farmhouse

lactose-intolerant: unable to digest lactose, a sugar found in dairy products

linguists: people who study languages and their structure

looms: wooden frames used for weaving

medicine bundles: collections of crushed plants, pollens, and pieces of stone from the four sacred mountains

migrated: moved from one place and settled in another place

mutton: meat from sheep

nomadic: people who move from place to place rather than settling in one area

ochre: an earthy pigment varying from light yellow to brown or red

powwows: American Indian events that feature traditional music, dancing, and singing

prayersticks: brightly colored, decorated sticks used to make offerings to the spirit world

pronunciation: a way of speaking a word

Pueblo: a farming-based American Indian group who live in New Mexico and Arizona

pueblo: a flat-roofed, connected building made from dried mud

reservation: land set apart by the federal government for use by an American Indian group

spindlewhorls: small wheels used to regulate the speed of spinning wheels

sumac: a shrub whose leaves are used for tanning and dying

supernatural: of, relating to, or seeming to come from a god

treaty: a formal agreement between two or more states regarding relations such as peace, trade, or land ownership

INDEX

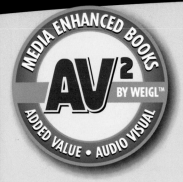

Log on to www.av2books.com

AV² by Weigl brings you media enhanced books that support active learning. Go to www.av2books.com, and enter the special code found on page 2 of this book. You will gain access to enriched and enhanced content that supplements and complements this book. Content includes video, audio, weblinks, quizzes, a slide show, and activities.

AV² Online Navigation

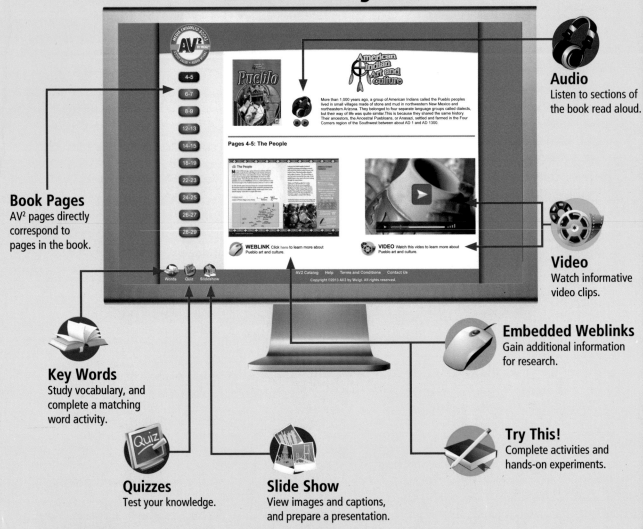

Audio
Listen to sections of the book read aloud.

Book Pages
AV² pages directly correspond to pages in the book.

Video
Watch informative video clips.

Key Words
Study vocabulary, and complete a matching word activity.

Embedded Weblinks
Gain additional information for research.

Try This!
Complete activities and hands-on experiments.

Quizzes
Test your knowledge.

Slide Show
View images and captions, and prepare a presentation.

AV² was built to bridge the gap between print and digital. We encourage you to tell us what you like and what you want to see in the future.

Sign up to be an AV² Ambassador at www.av2books.com/ambassador.

Due to the dynamic nature of the Internet, some of the URLs and activities provided as part of AV² by Weigl may have changed or ceased to exist. AV² by Weigl accepts no responsibility for any such changes. All media enhanced books are regularly monitored to update addresses and sites in a timely manner. Contact AV² by Weigl at 1-866-649-3445 or av2books@weigl.com with any questions, comments, or feedback.